W9-BLI-590

White House

by R.J. Bailey

Bullfrog Books

Ideas for Parents and Teachers

Bullfrog Books let children practice reading informational text at the earliest reading levels. Repetition, familiar words, and photo labels support early readers.

Before Reading

- Discuss the cover photo. What does it tell them?

- Look at the picture glossary together. Read and discuss the words.

Read the Book

- "Walk" through the book and look at the photos. Let the child ask questions. Point out the photo labels.

- Read the book to the child, or have him or her read independently.

After Reading

- Prompt the child to think more. Ask: Have you ever been to the White House? Did you go on a tour?

Bullfrog Books are published by Jump!
5357 Penn Avenue South
Minneapolis, MN 55419
www.jumplibrary.com

Library of Congress Cataloging-in-Publication Data

Names: Bailey, R. J., author.
Title: White House / by R.J. Bailey.
Description: Minneapolis, MN: Jump!, Inc., 2017.
Series: Hello, America! | "Bullfrog books."
Includes index. | Audience: Grades K to 3.
Audience: Ages 5 to 8.
Identifiers: LCCN 2016011854 (print)
LCCN 2016014176 (ebook)
ISBN 9781620313527 (hard cover: alk. paper)
ISBN 9781624963995 (e-book)
Subjects: LCSH: White House (Washington, D.C.)
—Juvenile literature. | Washington (D.C.)—
Buildings, structures, etc.—Juvenile literature.
Classification: LCC F204.W5 B35 2017 (print)
LCC F204.W5 (ebook) | DDC 975.3—dc23
LC record available at http://lccn.loc.gov/2016011854

Editor: Kirsten Chang
Series Designer: Ellen Huber
Book Designer: Molly Ballanger
Photo Researcher: Kirsten Chang

Photo Credits: Adobe Stock, cover; Alamy, 5, 7, 10–11, 23tl; Corbis, 8–9, 16–17, 17, 20–21, 23bl, 23br; Getty, 3, 4, 6–7, 12–13, 14, 18, 19, 22, 23tr; Shutterstock, 1, 15, 24.

Printed in the United States of America at Corporate Graphics in North Mankato, Minnesota.

Table of Contents

The President's House

The White House is in Washington, D.C.

Family lives here, too.
Even the pets!

The president works here.

Where?

The Oval Office.

It is in the West Wing.

The White House
has 132 rooms. Wow!

The East Room
is the largest.

It is for big events.

The president hosts world leaders.

They eat in the dining room.

Some rooms are for fun.
One room is for movies.

14

Another is for bowling. Strike!

The White House
has a big yard.

Look! Flowers!

It's the Rose Garden.

The president gives
speeches here.

What's that?
A helicopter!

It lands on the lawn.
The president gets out.

19

Welcome home!

The Oval Office

American flag

president's chair

president's desk

president's seal

Picture Glossary

East Room
The biggest room in the White House; it is for meetings, dinners, and concerts.

Washington, D.C.
The capital of the United States in the District of Columbia.

Rose Garden
A garden near the Oval Office; often used for speeches.

West Wing
The part of the White House where the Oval Office and other offices are located.

Index

To Learn More

Learning more is as easy as 1, 2, 3.

1) Go to www.factsurfer.com

2) Enter "WhiteHouse" into the search box.

3) Click the "Surf" button to see a list of websites.

With factsurfer.com, finding more information is just a click away.

24